A Pirate's Life

by John Hamilton

Visit us at
www.abdopublishing.com

Published by ABDO Publishing Company, 4940 Viking Drive, Suite 622, Edina, Minnesota 55435.

Printed in the United States.

Editors: Sue Hamilton/Tad Bornhoft
Graphic Design: John Hamilton
Cover Design: Neil Klinepier
Cover Illustration: *Taking the Whydah*, ©1998 Don Maitz; *Pegleg*, ©1996 Don Maitz
Interior Photos and Illustrations: p 1 *Caught Nipping*, ©1997 Don Maitz; p 3 *Dead Men Tell No Tales*, ©2003 Don Maitz; p 4 *Pirates of the Caribbean: The Curse of the Black Pearl* one-sheet, courtesy Walt Disney Pictures; p 5 *Which Shall be Captain*, Howard Pyle; p 7 *Taking the Whydah*, ©1998 Don Maitz; p 8 bone saw, Corbis; p 9 *Mindin' the Stores*, ©1999 Don Maitz; p 11 *Captain Rednose*, ©1996 Don Maitz; p 12 (top) *Barrel of Fun*, ©2002 Don Maitz; (bottom) hardtack, courtesy National Maritime Museum, London; p 13 (top) rat, Corbis; (bottom) scurvy treatment, Corbis; p 14 (top) *Marooned*, Howard Pyle; (bottom) pirate walking the plank, Howard Pyle; p 15 (top) cat-o'-nine-tails, courtesy National Maritime Museum, London; (bottom) hanging scene from *Pirates of the Caribbean: The Curse of the Black Pearl*, courtesy Walt Disney Pictures; p 16 pirate counting gold, Mariners' Museum; p 17 (top) cursed gold piece, courtesy Walt Disney Pictures; (bottom) *Pirate Banking*, ©2002 Don Maitz; p 18 (top) dog with keys, courtesy Walt Disney Pictures; (bottom) Captain Barbossa's monkey, courtesy Walt Disney Pictures; p 19 *Paully the Parrot*, ©1996 Don Maitz; p 21 map, Mariners' Museum; p 22 *Hanging by a Thread*, ©1998 Don Maitz; p 23 *Pirates Abroad*, ©2004 Don Maitz; p 24 detail from *Forty Thieves*, ©1991 Don Maitz; p 25 pirates await order to attack, Mary Evans Picture Library; p 26 *Shady Pirate*, ©2005 Don Maitz; p 27 *Foulbottom the Parrot*, ©2001 Don Maitz; p 28 Davy Jones from *Pirates of the Caribbean: Dead Man's Chest*, courtesy Walt Disney Pictures; p 30 *Up the Anchor*, ©2002 Don Maitz; p 31 pirate standing on deck, Howard Pyle; p 32 *Raging at the Moon*, ©2002 Don Maitz.

Library of Congress Cataloging-in-Publication Data

Hamilton, John, 1959-
  A pirate's life / John Hamilton.
    p. cm. -- (Pirates)
  Includes index.
  ISBN-13: 978-1-59928-762-1
  ISBN-10: 1-59928-762-5
  1. Pirates--Juvenile literature. I. Title.

G535.H255 2007
910.4'5--dc22

2006032025

Contents

DEAD MEN TELL NO TALES

A Grim Reality

When people think of pirates, many images come to mind: swashbuckling heroes dueling with cutlasses, fast sloops armed with blistering cannons, the Jolly Roger, eye patches, parrots, peg legs, plus buried treasure chests filled with glittering prizes.

Our popular culture has fed and nurtured this romantic image of piracy for hundreds of years, from Captain Charles Johnson's 1724 book *A General History of the Robberies and Murders of the Most Notorious Pyrates*, to 2003's *Pirates of the Caribbean: The Curse of the Black Pearl*, in which actor Johnny Depp single-handedly turned the pirate genre on its head with his rollicking depiction of Captain Jack Sparrow.

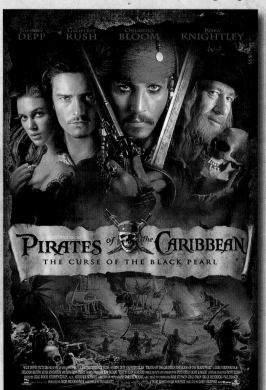

The reality of piracy was not so fun, and certainly not glorious. The life of a buccaneer was filled with violence, filth, uncertainty, and brutality. It was a hard life, filled with tough men. Life at sea was uncomfortable and unpredictable. Danger was always close at hand, followed by near-certain injury or death.

Still, we love our pirates. To escape the drudgery of modern life, it's fun to imagine yourself on a treasure-filled tropical island, or standing on the deck of a man-of-war, giving the order to attack. Yo ho!

Left: A lobby poster for the 2003 film *Pirates of the Caribbean.*
Facing page: Which Shall be Captain by Howard Pyle.

Ship's Crew

"They came out of the blue. They attacked, they looted, and they vanished."
—David Cordingly, *Under the Black Flag*

A pirate ship required many people, all working together, to sail smoothly. Most were young men in their 20s, from seaports all over Europe and the Americas. Many were former navy sailors, or merchant seamen who joined the pirate ranks after being raided. They came from many nations, but shared common traits. They had sunburned skin and hardened muscles from working long hours on deck. They had "sea legs," a kind of rolling gait needed to keep their balance on deck in rough water. They had distinctive clothing, and a way of talking that was difficult for landlubbers to understand. Most were common seamen, but some performed special tasks.

Captain

Pirate crews were some of the first democracies in the world. Many pirates came from military ships that were commanded by cruel captains. Pirates refused to tolerate this harsh treatment. They voted for captains from within their own ranks, giving the job to experienced sailors who could lead men into battle with daring and courage. Captains had to be skilled navigators and cunning warriors. Many were tough and utterly ruthless. Most of all, they had to command missions that brought plenty of booty to be shared by the crew. If a pirate captain didn't produce results that made his men happy, he could easily be voted out of a job. Unsuccessful captains might find themselves flung overboard, or marooned on a desert island, doomed to watch their ships sail away without them.

Facing page: Taking the Whydah by Don Maitz.

Quartermaster

On a pirate ship, the quartermaster was often second in command, similar to the first mate of a regular sailing vessel. His job was to distribute goods like food and gunpowder. He decided who did chores, and who was punished for wrongdoing. He also made sure treasure was divided fairly among the crew.

Carpenter

The carpenter was a very important person on a ship. He fixed hulls and masts that became damaged from battles or storms. It took a highly skilled carpenter to keep a ship afloat.

Boatswain

The boatswain (pronounced "bos'n") was a junior officer who had various duties, including attending to a ship's rigging and anchors, and making sure the deck was kept clear.

Master Gunner

Aiming and firing whole banks of cannons was a skill that took years to perfect. With experienced gunners on board, a pirate ship could fire devastating broadsides at the enemy.

Surgeon

Most pirate crews used cooks or carpenters to amputate badly injured limbs. When surgeons were discovered on plundered vessels, they were often pressed into service. Surgeons used special knives, such as bone saws, to amputate limbs or remove bullets. Quick work was needed to reduce infection, which was a killer in the days before antibiotics. Sailors with amputated limbs could be fitted with hook hands or peg legs. Many amputees became cooks, such as Long John Silver in Robert Louis Stevenson's *Treasure Island*.

Powder Monkey

A powder monkey was a crew member who loaded and cleaned the ship's cannons. Boys as young as 12 were often kidnapped and pressed into service as powder monkeys.

Cabin Boy

The cabin boy was a young boy, or a new crew member, who ran errands, cleaned cabins, and generally helped the captain with the day-to-day drudgery of running a ship.

Above: A 17th-century bone saw. *Facing page: Mindin' the Stores* by Don Maitz.

Life Aboard Ship

The glamorous, swashbuckling heroes of *Captain Blood* or *Pirates of the Caribbean* would be shocked if they ever set foot on a real pirate ship. For starters, they'd probably be knocked over by the smell, a combination of sweat, dead fish, rotting food, and animal waste. Fresh water was a luxury aboard ships, so baths were few and far between. Descending below deck, the smell got worse. Cramped quarters and a lack of fresh air made for a nose-wrinkling stench, especially when sailing in the stifling heat of the tropics.

A pirate crew lived a hard and dangerous life. Smell was the least of their worries. Storm-tossed seas led to broken bones or other serious injuries, not to mention seasickness. Battles sometimes resulted in severed limbs, eyes being shot out, cracked skulls, or slit throats. Pirates also fought among themselves, often in drunken rages that turned violent. In between these episodes, pirates faced the enemy of sailors everywhere: extreme boredom. To pass the time, they made up clever songs called chanties, some of which are still sung by sailors today.

Many buccaneers started out as honest sailors, but were pressed into service by pirates. That means they were kidnapped and forced to lead piratical lives. But to some, it was a step up, an escape from the harsh lives of military seamen, such as those who served in the British Royal Navy.

Facing page:
Captain Rednose
by Don Maitz.

There were no bathrooms aboard pirate ships. When nature called, sailors used heads, or "seats of ease." They were also called jardins, which was French for "gardens." The head was a simple hole cut in the deck planking on a ship's bow (front). Lacking any kind of privacy, sailors dropped their pants, sat on the hole, and did their business into the sea. (Despite its name, the poop deck was simply the highest and rear-most deck on a ship, not a place for sailors to relieve themselves.)

Pirates slept in any comfortable spot they could find. Usually, only the captain had a cabin with his own bunk, or bed. For the rest of the crew, there wasn't much space inside the ship's hull. A sack of grain might make a comfortable mattress. Some pirates slept on hammocks strung between wooden beams. When the seas were calm, many slept on deck where the air was fresh.

One of the reasons pirates drank so much alcohol was that it was easier to store than water. Fresh water often developed an algae scum, especially on long sea voyages. Beer or rum could be added to water to make it taste better. Grog was a pirate favorite, made by mixing water, rum, and spices such as cinnamon or lemon.

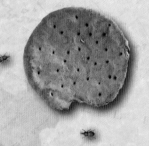

Pirate food varied greatly, depending on what part of the world the ship sailed. Sometimes local fruits and vegetables were brought aboard. These items were quick to rot, however. Live animals, such as goats and pigs, were often kept below deck. Livestock could be milked, or eaten as fresh meat. More often, however, pirates ate a combination of dried meat and a tough biscuit called hardtack. Made of water and flour (and sometimes lard), hardtack was often infested with small beetles called weevils.

Top: Barrel of Fun by Don Maitz. *Above:* Hardtack was a biscuit made of flour and water. It was often infested with weevils.

Weevils were not the only pests to stow away aboard pirate ships. Poisonous spiders and scorpions were commonly found in crates of food, or bundles of firewood collected from shore, especially in the tropics. Fleas were a constant irritant. They lived in the seams of the men's clothes, or in their hair.

The itching could be unbearable. Bigger vermin, too, plagued most sailing vessels. Rats infested the holds of ships, feasting on stored provisions. They also gnawed on wood, rope, or anything else they could bite with their razor-sharp teeth, including the sailors. From time to time, the crew went on rat-hunting expeditions to keep the rodent population under control. One Spanish galleon, traveling from Europe to the Caribbean, recorded killing over 4,000 rats during the trip.

Rats and fleas resulted in disease, including plague. Intestinal diseases, such as cholera and dysentery, were common among sailors. Mosquito-born malaria was often picked up in the tropics. Another common shipboard disease was scurvy, which resulted in exhaustion, loss of teeth, and internal bleeding. Scurvy was caused by a lack of vitamin C in the crew's meager diet. By 1800, British doctors realized they could prevent the deadly disease by feeding sailors fresh vegetables, or lemons and limes. This is why British sailors after this time were often called "limeys."

With so much misery and discomfort, it is a wonder anybody became a sailor. The truth is, many sailors had no choice. They took to the sea to escape crushing poverty, or were pressed into service against their will. But many pirates relished the freedom of the open water and limitless horizons. The chance to make their fortune, and live a life of ease, made the hardships of pirate life worthwhile.

Above: The destructive brown rat spread disease. *Left:* A British ship's doctor gives lemons to sailors stricken with scurvy. Vitamin C in citrus fruits prevented the dread disease.

Punishment

Pirates were notorious for the cruelty they inflicted on their innocent victims. They were also quick to dole out punishment to their crew mates if the rules were broken. Pirate captains decided who got punished, but the quartermaster actually carried out the order. This prevented too much power resting in the hands of the captain. If the punishment seemed unfair, the quartermaster could refuse the order, and the crew could then vote for a new captain.

Walking the Plank

Hollywood and popular fiction created the myth of pirates forcing their victims to walk the plank. Pirate captain Bartholomew Roberts may have forced some captives to walk to a watery grave. But most pirates simply gave the order to "heave to," which meant the poor victims were unceremoniously tossed overboard. Some captives were lashed to a mast and used as target practice before their bodies were sent to Davy Jones' locker.

Cat-O'-Nine-Tails

The cat-o'-nine-tails was a whip commonly found on sailing ships. It was a nasty device, made of cow or horse hide, with nine lines. Sometimes the

Above right: A Howard Pyle illustration of an unfortunate sailor marooned on a desert island.

Left: In real life, pirates seldom walked the plank. Painting by Howard Pyle.

lines were knotted at the end, or had sharp wire or steel balls attached to make the lashes even more painful. Flogging was a cruel, but not unusual, punishment aboard sailing ships of the pirate era. The most severe punishment was 39 lashes, or strokes, of the whip. This was called Moses' Law. According to the Bible's Old Testament, 40 lashes was the amount needed to kill a man. Therefore, 39 lashes was the most punishment you could give without handing out a death sentence. In practice, a person could easily die from less, depending on the kind of whip and the skill of the person wielding it. Whips were designed to tear the flesh off victims' bodies. If that didn't kill them, infection often did.

Above: The dreaded cat-o'-nine-tails.

Keelhauling

Keelhauling was a particularly gruesome form of punishment, equal to a death sentence. Pirates seldom employed it, but sailors aboard British Royal Navy ships were sometimes keelhauled. A rope was passed underneath the ship, then one end tied to the victim's hands. He was then tossed overboard and dragged under the boat to the other side. If the victim didn't drown first, he was almost certainly torn apart by the sharp barnacles that covered the bottom of the ship's hull.

Marooning

This was a very common punishment among pirates. Victims were simply left to die on a tiny deserted island, usually with no water, food, or shelter. Sometimes they were given a pistol with a single shot—to kill themselves when they couldn't stand it anymore.

Below: Captain Jack Sparrow faces execution by hanging in *Pirates of the Caribbean: The Curse of the Black Pearl.*

Hanging

Unless they were granted a pardon, most pirates faced the ultimate penalty—death by hanging. The strangling process took several gruesome minutes. Because ropes were made from the hemp plant, hanged pirates were said to "dance the hempen jig."

Treasure

The lust for wealth was in every pirate's black heart. Without the chance to plunder treasure, there was no reason to risk death by turning to piracy. Luckily, there was plenty of treasure to go around, especially on the Spanish Main of the 16th and 17th centuries. Enormous galleons bloated with precious cargo regularly crossed the Atlantic Ocean, heading home after filling their hulls with gold, silver, and jewels taken from the rich mines of the Americas. These ships, and the ports where the treasure was collected and stored, were prime targets for many pirates.

Pieces of eight and doubloons were common Spanish currency in the age of piracy. A silver piece of eight was like an American dollar, but instead of being worth 100 pennies, it was worth eight "reales" ("royals"). A single piece of eight could be cut into four sections (quarters), or even eight separate pieces, and still retain its value, since it was made of pure silver. A doubloon was a gold coin that was worth several times that of a piece of eight. In addition to gold coins, the Spanish also forged gold bars and gold chains. The chains could be snipped off one link at a time to pay for goods and services.

Gold does not corrode in salt water. When today's treasure hunters find the wrecks of Spanish galleons, the gold they pull from the sea is as shiny and bright as the day it went to Davy Jones' locker.

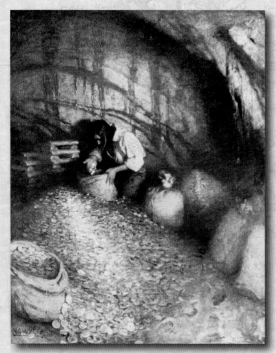

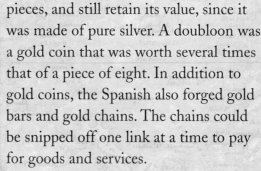

Left: Kneeling atop a mound of golden doubloons, a pirate counts his hoard of treasure in a secret cave.

When dividing their plunder, or booty, some pirates got bigger shares than others. The quartermaster was responsible for distributing the spoils. The captain, quartermaster, carpenter, and master gunner usually received a larger part of the treasure. Surgeons also commonly received extra pay for their valued services. Besides gold, silver, and jewels, pirate treasure included merchandise such as silk, coffee, sugar cane, or plundered weapons. Slaves were also traded.

It is a common myth that most pirates hoarded their wealth, burying treasure chests on remote desert islands. Some pirates did indeed bury treasure. Even today, people continue searching for the lost treasures of William Kidd, Henry Morgan, and the dreaded Blackbeard. But in reality, most treasure was never buried. Pirates sailed to port and spent their ill-gotten gains almost as quickly as they could steal it.

Above: A cursed gold coin plays a prominent role in the 2003 blockbuster film *Pirates of the Caribbean: The Curse of the Black Pearl.* *Below: Pirate Banking* by artist Don Maitz.

Pirate Pets

Pirate mascots are as common in fictional accounts as peg legs and eye patches. Long John Silver kept a caged parrot called Cap'n Flint in Robert Louis Stevenson's *Treasure Island*. But did real pirates keep parrots as pets? We don't know for sure. The birds were a colorful novelty and could be taught to speak. Some pirates, returning from tropical ports, may have kept parrots as souvenirs. David Cordingly, in *Under the Black Flag*, notes that parrots and parakeets were sometimes used as bribes. In 1582, pirate captain Stephen Haynes gave two parrots to the servant of a high-ranking British official. There are also several references to parrots in nonfiction books written during the age of pirates. In 1676, English buccaneer William Dampier described parrots he saw during a voyage to the West Indies: "Their color was yellow and red, very coarsely mixed; and they would prate very prettily and there was scarce a man but what sent aboard one or two of them."

Some pirates may have kept pet monkeys, but they were probably more trouble than they were worth. Dogs, too, might have found their way onto pirate vessels. But dogs need meat to survive, a precious commodity during long sea voyages. If a pirate owned a dog, he probably kept it safe at home. On the other hand, dogs or cats would come in handy to kill the many mice and rats that infested sailing vessels.

Top right: A dog holds the keys to the jail in Disney's 2003 film *Pirates of the Caribbean: The Curse of the Black Pearl*.
Left: The cursed pet monkey of Captain Barbossa, from *Pirates of the Caribbean*.
Facing page: Paully the Parrot, by artist Don Maitz.

Arr, Matey!

Pirates had their own unique way of talking. To an outsider, pirate chatter could be very difficult to understand. In their vocabulary, pirates used many unique nautical terms and slang related to the sailing life:

Ahoy!—Hello.

Aloft—A high part of the ship, such as the top of the mast.

Arr!—Yes, or aye.

Astern—Toward the back of the ship.

Avast!—A command to stop.

Batten down—To secure hatches and loose items on deck and within the hull.

Belay that!—Stop that!

Bilge rat—A scoundrel.

Booty—Plundered treasure or trade goods.

Bow—The forward part of a ship.

Broadside—Firing all the guns on one side of the ship.

Cackle fruit—Chicken eggs.

Corsair—A pirate, especially from the Mediterranean Sea.

Dance the hempen jig—Strangling to death while hanging.

Davy Jones' locker—The bottom of the sea.

Deadlights—Eyes.

Devil's jig—To hang.

Feed the fish—To be thrown overboard.

Handsomely—Quickly.

Hearties (Me hearties)—Brave and loyal sailors.

Hornswoggle—To cheat.

Jolly Roger—A pirate flag.

Line—A rope used aboard a ship.

Lubber—A clumsy seaman.

Man-of-war—A navy ship equipped for warfare.

Mate—A friend.

Monkey—A small cannon.

Oggin—The ocean.

Pox—Disease.

Savvy?—Do you understand?

Sea rat—A pirate.

Scurvy dog—A scoundrel.

Scuttle—To intentionally sink a ship.

Shiver me timbers!—An expression of surprise. When a ship was hit by cannon fire, the wooden hull could be felt shaking.

Squall—A sudden storm or gust of violent wind.

Swab—A low-ranking seaman.

Swallow the anchor—To retire from piracy.

Sweet trade—Piracy.

Timbers—The wooden framework of a ship.

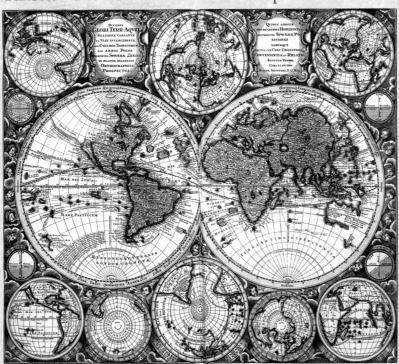

Left: A map of the known world in 1700, during the Golden Age of Piracy.

Women Pirates

The vast majority of pirates were men, but there were several notable exceptions. Some women proved themselves equal to any man, both in battle and in commanding sea vessels. One of the most successful pirates in history was a Chinese woman named Cheng Yih Sao, or simply Mrs. Cheng. In the early 1800s, she was the terror of the South China Sea. At one point she commanded a force of more than 50,000 pirates.

Grace O'Malley was born in Ireland around 1530. When she was a young girl she went to sea, blending in with the men sailors by cutting her hair short. As a woman, she became a bold and fearless pirate leader.

By far the most famous women pirates were Anne Bonny and Mary Read. Together, they cruised the Caribbean in the early 1700s. They were crew members of pirate John Rackham, nicknamed Calico Jack. They disguised themselves by dressing in men's clothes and, like Grace O'Malley, cutting their hair short. Armed with pistols and cutlasses, they fought as well as most men. In 1720, the two women pirates, along with Calico Jack, were captured by a privateer working for the British Royal Navy. At their trial, they were all found guilty and sentenced to be hanged. But the two women claimed they were both pregnant, and their execution was temporarily suspended. Shortly after the trial, while in prison, Mary Read contracted a fever and died. It is unknown whether Anne Bonny gave birth to her child, or what happened to her afterwards.

Facing page: Pirates Abroad by artist Don Maitz. *Below: Hanging by a Thread* by Don Maitz.

Black Pirates

A pirate crew included people from many different ethnic backgrounds and nationalities. The majority were white men from English-speaking countries. A great many pirates, however, were black men.

One witness who was aboard a vessel that was attacked by the pirate Bartholomew Roberts in 1721 reported that the pirate ship was manned by 180 white men and 48 blacks. A second pirate ship accompanying Roberts included 100 whites and 40 blacks. In 1722, Captain Chaloner Ogle of Great Britain rounded up the survivors of Roberts' crew after a battle in which the dread pirate was fatally wounded. Captain Ogle reported that the remaining pirates included 187 white men and 75 black men.

Besides Bartholomew Roberts, other pirate captains employed black crewmen as well. Pirates Edward England, Richard Frowd, and Augustin Blanco all had crews with racial mixes similar to Roberts'. Many other pirate ships on the Spanish Main undoubtedly had black men serving as crew members. Historians are busy trying to answer several questions about black pirates. Who were these men? Were they treated any differently from their white crew mates?

Some people think that black pirates were treated equally. Even though pirates could be bloodthirsty and cruel, they were often fair-minded sailors who went against the customs of their era. It's possible they welcomed escaped slaves from the plantations of the Caribbean

Below: A detail from artist Don Maitz' *Forty Thieves,* which shows a black pirate manning a small cannon.

islands, or from slave ships traveling from Africa to the Americas. Joining a pirate crew might be one way for these desperate souls to find their freedom, or at least seek shelter from the slave owners hunting them down. Bartholomew Roberts had a reputation for freeing slaves from ships he plundered, and offering them positions among his crew.

In reality, the vast majority of pirates were just as prejudiced as other people of their time. Captured slaves were often treated as valuable commodities to be traded, or used aboard pirate ships to perform menial tasks. Even Bartholomew Roberts was quick to use slaves, or even have them killed, if it served his purposes.

Above: Pirates, including several black crew members, wait for their captain to give the order to attack a fat prize.

Pirate Clothes

When pirates went to sea, they brought the clothes on their backs. There were no uniforms for pirates. Their clothing was practical for the kind of rough work they performed at sea.

In many Hollywood films, pirates dressed in a stereotypical fashion. Pirate captains wore fancy longcoats, draped over ruffled shirts and silk vests, and topped their heads with powdered wigs and tricorn hats adorned with feathers. In reality, pirates dressed in much simpler clothes for day-to-day sailing action. Captains distinguished themselves from their crews by wearing a coat, but it was usually a plain blue "sea coat" that reached to the knees, or slightly lower.

Facing page: Foulbottom the Parrot by artist Don Maitz. *Below: Shady Pirate* by Don Maitz.

Regular sailors wore woolen coats in gray or blue. In rough seas, they also wore canvas jackets that had been waterproofed with a coating of tar or wax. On their legs, they wore woolen pants, or canvas breeches. Especially when sailing in the tropical heat, many sailors went bare chested, or wore a simple white shirt.

On their heads, pirates shielded themselves from the tropical sun by wearing bicorn or tricorn hats, or woolen caps. Colorful head scarves or bandannas were also common.

When they worked on the slippery decks aboard ship, pirates usually went barefoot. They saved their shoes, and any other fancy clothes they owned, for visits ashore, where they hoped for a chance to impress any lady friends they happened to meet.

Pirate Lore

Pirates were a superstitious lot. They also loved to tell stories of the sea. One of the most famous tales was that of Davy Jones. When a sailor was said to go to Davy Jones' locker, it meant he died or was killed, and his body sank to the bottom of the sea.

Davy Jones was most likely the devil, or a kind of supernatural creature. His story has been passed down for hundreds of years by fearful sailors. In Tobias Smollett's 1751 novel *The Adventures of Peregrine Pickle*, Davy Jones is

described as a shape-changing demon who foretells doom:

This same Davy Jones, according to sailors, is the fiend that presides over all the evil spirits of the deep, and is often seen in various shapes, perching among the rigging on the eve of hurricuanes, ship-wrecks, and other disasters to which sea-faring life is exposed, warning the devoted wretch of death and woe.

In the 2006 film *Pirates of the Caribbean: Dead Man's Chest*, Davy Jones is the villain of the story. He is a half-man, half-sea creature, with a full beard of wriggling octopus legs and a crab claw for a hand.

Left: Bill Nighy as Davy Jones, in Walt Disney's *Pirates of the Caribbean: Dead Man's Chest.*

Left: A kraken attacks a helpless sea vessel.

A kraken was a legendary sea monster, most likely a giant squid or octopus, that attacked ships and dragged poor sailors to their doom. There are accounts of krakens attacking in all the world's oceans, but their origin may have been off the coasts of Norway and Iceland.

There is some truth to the legend of the kraken. Real giant squid can grow up to 50 feet (15m) long. It's easy to imagine a sailor spotting one of these great beasts and then making up a wild story to exaggerate the facts. Everyone loves a tall tale.

Another favorite sea tale is the strange story of the Flying Dutchman. According to the legend, which is hundreds of years old, the Flying Dutchman is a ghost ship, doomed to wander the oceans for all eternity. Its captain, a Dutchman by the name of Van der Decken, lost a game of dice with the devil. He and his crew were then cursed never to find a safe harbor for their ship.

Below: A sighting of the ghostly Flying Dutchman.

The phantom vessel is usually seen in the distance, sailing silently past. Some accounts say the ship glows with an eerie, ghostly light. Its appearance is often considered by alarmed sailors to be a sign of imminent doom.

Glossary

Booty
A pirate word meaning treasure, or plunder.

Broadside
When a warship simultaneously fires all its cannons on one side.

Buccaneers
Men who raided and captured ships, especially off the Spanish coasts of America during the 17th and 18th centuries.

Caribbean
The islands and area of the Caribbean Sea, roughly the area between Florida and South and Central America.

Corsair
Another term for pirate. "Corsair" usually refers to pirates of the Mediterranean Sea, working off the north coast of Africa.

Cutlass
A short, curved sword having a single sharp edge, often used by seamen.

Golden Age of Piracy
Roughly the years 1660 to 1740, the era when piracy was at its peak, especially along the coast of colonial America and in the Caribbean. Many former privateers, put out of work as peace spread across Europe, turned to piracy. The lack of a strong, central colonial government led to poor protection of ships at sea, at a time when many vessels carried valuables across the Atlantic Ocean.

Keel

The keel is the stiff center, or spine, of a ship that runs from bow to stern (front to back). It was often made of a hardwood, like teak. The rest of the ship's hull is built upon and supported by the keel.

Letter of Marque

Official government document granting a ship captain permission to use his personal armed vessel for capturing and raiding ships of another country. Used by governments to expand their naval forces at a time of war.

Man-of-War

A large sailing warship armed with many cannons. These ships were used on the front line of a battle.

Privateer

A ship, or its captain and crew, operating under a letter of marque. A country issued letters of marque to permit the raiding of ships from specified countries that it had engaged in war. The captain and crew were paid out of any booty they took from the ships they attacked. Also known as "gentlemen pirates."

Sloop

A fast sailing vessel with a single mast. Outfitted for war, it had a single gun deck with 10 to 18 cannons.

Left: A pirate stands on the deck of his ship in heavy seas. His latest victim is a burning hulk slowly sinking behind him. Painting by Howard Pyle.

Index

A
Adventures of Peregrine Pickle, The 28
Africa 25
Americas 6, 16, 25
Atlantic Ocean 16

B
Bible 15
Blackbeard 17
Blanco, Augustin 24
Boatswain 8
Bonny, Anne 22

C
cabin boy 8
Calico Jack (*see* Rackham, John)
Cap'n Flint 18
captain 6, 8, 12, 14, 17, 26
Captain Blood 10
Caribbean Sea 13, 22, 24
carpenter 8, 17
cat 18

cat-o'-nine-tails 14
chanty 10
Cheng, Mrs. (Cheng Yih Sao) 22
cholera 13
Cordingly, David 6, 18
cutlass 4, 22

D
Dampier, William 18
dance the hempen jig 15
Davy Jones' locker 14, 16, 20, 28
Depp, Johnny 4
der Decken, Van 29
devil 28, 29
dog 18
doubloon 16
dysentery 13

E
England, Edward 24
Europe 6, 13
eye patch 4, 18

F
fleas 12, 13
Flying Dutchman 29
Frowd, Richard 24

G
General History of the Robberies and Murders of the Most Notorious Pyrates, A 4
Great Britain 24
grog 12

H
hanging 15
hardtack 12
Haynes, Stephen 18
head 12
Hollywood, CA 14, 26

I
Iceland 29
Ireland 22

J
Johnson, Charles 4
Jolly Roger 4, 20
Jones, Davy 14, 16, 20, 28

K
keelhauling 15
Kidd, William 17
kraken 29

L
limey 13

M
malaria 13
man-of-war 4, 21
marooning 15
master gunner 8, 17
Mediterranean Sea 20
monkey 18
Morgan, Henry 17
Moses' Law 15

N
Norway 29

O
Ogle, Chaloner 24
Old Testament 15
O'Malley, Grace 22

P
parrot 4, 18
peg leg 4, 8, 18
pieces of eight 16
Pirates of the Caribbean: Dead Man's Chest 28
Pirates of the Caribbean: The Curse of the Black Pearl 10
plague 13
plank, walking the 14
poop deck 12
powder monkey 8

Q
quartermaster 8, 14, 17

R
Rackham, John (Calico Jack) 22
rat 13
Read, Mary 22
Roberts, Bartholomew 14, 24, 25
Royal Navy 10, 15, 22

S
scurvy 13
Silver, Long John 8, 18
slaves 24, 25
sloop 4
Smollett, Tobias 28
South China Sea 22
Spanish Main 16, 24
Sparrow, Jack 4
squid, giant 29
Stevenson, Robert Louis 8, 18
surgeon 8, 17

T
Treasure Island 8, 18

U
Under the Black Flag 6, 18

V
vitamin C 13

W
weevils 12
West Indies 18

Raging at the Moon by Don Maitz.